Interpreting Language Models

A Guide to Explainable AI Techniques for Transformers

Taylor Royce

DEDICATION

To the inquisitive minds who want to comprehend the complex mechanisms of artificial intelligence and to those who think that the keys to releasing its full potential lie in interpretability and transparency.

This book is intended for engineers, researchers, and innovators who are committed to improving the ethical, comprehensible, and reliable nature of AI. I hope it motivates you to create self-explanatory systems in addition to smarter ones.

DISCLAIMER

This book's content is solely intended for informational and educational purposes. The correctness, completeness, and dependability of the information provided are not guaranteed by the author or publisher. Although every attempt has been taken to guarantee that the content is current and correct, methodologies, tools, and best practices may change due to the quick evolution of artificial intelligence and machine learning technologies.

The publisher and author disclaim all liability for any actions based on the information in this book, including but not limited to any losses, damages, or legal repercussions that may arise from using the material. When putting the methods and ideas covered into practice, readers are urged to use critical thinking skills and refer to other sources.

No software, tool, or service is recommended or endorsed in this book. Each and every brand name, service mark, and trademark belongs to its owner.

CONTENTS

ACKNOWLEDGMENTS

I want to express my sincere gratitude to everyone who helped me along the way when I was writing this book.

I want to express my gratitude to my family and friends for their unwavering support, tolerance, and comprehension throughout the many hours I spent researching and writing. Your confidence in me sustained me during the most trying times.

Your opinions and thoughts have been really helpful, colleagues and peers in the field of artificial intelligence. I appreciate you pushing my thinking, imparting your knowledge, and generating fresh concepts.

A particular thank you to the several academics and developers whose contributions to explainable AI, machine learning, and artificial intelligence served as the basis for this book. The future of technology is still being shaped by your contributions.

Lastly, I want to sincerely thank all of the people who have read this book. The advancement of the area is fueled by your curiosity about comprehending and enhancing AI. I sincerely hope that the information presented here will encourage and enable you on your own path.

CHAPTER 1

EXPLAINABILITY IS IMPORTANT—THE RISE OF THE TRANSFORMERS

Over the past ten years, artificial intelligence (AI) has advanced quickly, moving from simple rule-based systems to complex models that can diagnose illnesses, produce responses similar to those of a human, and even help in court. The emergence of transformer-powered large language models (LLMs), such as GPT, BERT, and their numerous variations, is one of the most groundbreaking developments. However, these models have a significant drawback: despite their incredible potency, they are infamously opaque.

This chapter explores why explainability is not only a desirable but also a necessary feature in AI, particularly in transformer-based systems. We discuss the differences between transformers, the effects of opacity, and the need of comprehending these systems for safety, accountability, and trust in a future where AI-driven judgments are becoming more and more prevalent.

1.1 AI's "Black Box Problem": Why LLMs Are Effective but Inconspicuous

The remarkable ability of transformer-based models, such as GPT-4 or BERT, to comprehend context, produce logical text, and execute multiple tasks without task-specific tuning has led to their widespread adoption. However, beneath the surface, they function using billions of parameters arranged in patterns that are incomprehensible to the human eye.

The phrase "black box" refers to models whose inner workings are obscured or unintelligible. The system generates an output based on the data you enter, but the logic behind that output is sometimes not even clear to the engineers who created the system. The following factors combine to provide this opaqueness:

- Complex architectures with feedforward computations and deeply layered layers of self-attention.

- Large datasets utilized for training, which are frequently confidential or proprietary.
- Emergent behavior that arises from scale and training dynamics but is not expressly coded.

Real-World Failures Due to AI Opacity

The repercussions can be severe if we are unable to comprehend the reasons behind the actions of AI systems. Here are some noteworthy instances:

- COMPAS Algorithm (U.S. Criminal Justice System): This proprietary algorithm was employed to estimate recidivism risk but was found to demonstrate racial prejudice. Judges depended on it, but the process was hidden—leading to charges of "black-box justice."

- Google Photos Tagging Incident: Black people were mistakenly identified as gorillas by an AI image recognition model. Because of the system's opacity, developers were unable to identify the root cause or swiftly resolve it, which resulted in the temporary deactivation of the feature.

- Amazon's Employment Resource: It was discovered that an AI designed to sort resumes penalizes applications that contain the word "women's" (e.g., "women's chess club captain"). Gender bias was something it had learned from past data. The project was ultimately abandoned due to a lack of transparency in the decision-making process.

Opacity has societal, legal, and ethical ramifications and is not just a technical defect.

1.2 Transparency and Trust: Who Needs to Know How AI Makes Decisions?

Explainability is not limited to researchers in a world where AI is integrated into criminal justice, healthcare, financial services, and even the military. To guarantee that systems are utilized responsibly, fairly, and safely, a wide range of stakeholders must be aware of AI decisions.

Important Parties Requiring Explainability in AI:

- Regulators and Policymakers: Agencies such as the FDA, SEC, or European Commission need to understand how AI makes choices to assess if it complies with existing rules or if new regulations are needed.

- Final Users: Users must understand why an AI system made a choice, whether they are a customer who has had their loan application rejected or a clinician evaluating AI-assisted diagnosis.

- Engineers and Developers: When models' workings are unclear, debugging and system improvement turn into a guessing game rather than a scientific one.

- Managers of Risk and Executives: Business executives who want to incorporate AI into their processes must have faith in these systems. A lack of explainability increases responsibility and erodes trust.

Sectors Where Explainability Is Mission-Critical

- Healthcare: For clinical validation and malpractice prevention, AI diagnostics must be interpretable. When patients' lives are on the line, doctors cannot rely on vague recommendations.

- Finance: Transparency is necessary for fraud detection, credit rating, and investment forecasting. Legislation such as the Fair Credit Reporting Act must be followed by financial organizations.

To guarantee that they do not reinforce systemic biases, risk assessment instruments and facial recognition software must be transparent (Criminal Justice:).

- Autonomous Automobiles: We must ascertain why a self-driving car crashes. Future prevention and responsibility assessment may be hampered by decision-making that is difficult to explain.

- HR and Hiring Resources: Fair and impartial

employment decisions must be made by algorithms. Businesses run the danger of sustaining prejudice in the absence of explainability.

1.3 Explainable LLMs to Explainable ML: Why Conventional XAI Is Insufficient for Transformers

The goal of the long-running research field of explainable AI (XAI) is to improve the interpretability of models. Conventional methods like logistic regression, convolutional neural networks (CNNs), and decision trees have shown a reasonable level of success with LIME, SHAP, and feature significance graphs. Transformers, however, are a very different animal.

Why Conventional Approaches Fail

- The concept of high dimensionality: Transformers operate using attention weights and high-dimensional embeddings that are difficult to translate into notions that are understandable by humans.

- Contextual Complexity: LLMs take into account entire text sequences, which makes it challenging to assign output to a single input feature or token.

- Dependencies between layers: It can be challenging to track down a change in one token's embedding as it can ripple across dozens of layers and interact non-linearly with other tokens.

- Emergent behaviors include: At scale, transformers exhibit unprogrammed behaviors like reasoning and in-context learning. Conventional feature attribution is unable to account for these.

The Need for Techniques Particular to Transformers

New methods like these have emerged as a result of the need for explainability in transformers:

- A visual representation of the words that the model "attended" to during its predictions. This has drawbacks, though, because importance and attention are not always the same.

- Examining intermediate layers to see what linguistic or conceptual information is stored is known as "probing classifiers."

- Using interventions or ablations, layer attribution methods are used to determine which layers are primarily responsible for specific predictions.

- The goal of concept activation vectors, or CAVs, is to connect model choices to ideas that are understandable to humans.

None of these approaches offer a complete picture, and they are continually developing. However, they signal a move away from general XAI and toward domain-specific tools designed to handle the intricacies of transformer models.

1.4 The Path Ahead: Resources, Strategies, and Philosophy What and How This Book Will Cover

Explainability in AI is not merely a technological

endeavor—it is a philosophical and societal one. To achieve substantial progress, we need to migrate from a model-centric approach that values accuracy and efficiency, to a human-centric one that prioritizes clarity, trust, and usability.

Core Mindset Shifts Required:

- From Control to Collaboration: AI should not dictate decisions but aid people in making better ones. Explainable interactions are necessary for that.

- From Metrics to Meaning: End users don't care much about accuracy, F1 scores, or BLEU scores. What counts is whether they understand and trust the AI.

- From Opacity to Conversation: Models should be designed to answer questions about their reasoning—not just produce an output and move on.

Transitioning from a one-size-fits-all approach to contextual explainability:

What a layperson wants is not the same as what a regulator needs, therefore the type and degree of explanation that is needed may differ.

Topics This Book Will Cover:

- Innovative techniques for elucidating transformer choices.
- A critical evaluation of current instruments, such as saliency ratings, attention maps, and SHAP.
- A human-first approach for judging the value of explanations.
- Case studies that are sector-specific and demonstrate explainability in action.
- New developments in responsible AI and interpretable deep learning.

We must keep in mind this when we develop the next generation of intelligent systems: humans must make the decisions, even though models may make the predictions.

The transformer era has begun. It brings with it a strength and opacity never seen before. Explainability is now essential to moral, responsible, and successful AI; it is no longer a specialized issue. We must demand clarity in addition to performance in a world where algorithms are influencing our lives more and more. In order to make the computers of the future not only intelligent but also comprehensible, we will examine ways to illuminate the "black box" as we continue reading this book

CHAPTER 2

TRANSFORMER ANATOMY: WHAT ARE WE EXPLAINING?

We must first get a solid understanding of the actual functions of large language models (LLMs) before we can begin to interpret or explain them in any meaningful way. Transformers, the fundamental architecture of contemporary LLMs such as GPT, BERT, and T5, mark a change in both the conceptual underpinnings of how machines learn and produce language that is similar to that of humans as well as in processing capacity. Transformers are among the least understood systems by non-specialists, despite their sophistication.

Piece by piece, this chapter delves into the Transformer's architecture and operation. We aim to demystify the moving pieces by providing a conceptual map that grounds explainability efforts in something tangible, rather than burdening you with superfluous mathematics or technical language. It takes more than just academic knowledge to comprehend how transformers digest information. Interpreting their results, identifying problems, fostering trust, and judiciously implementing them in crucial areas are all crucial.

2.1 The Game of Encoder-Decoder

The encoder and the decoder are the two primary components of the original Transformer architecture, which was first presented in the groundbreaking work "Attention Is All You Need" by Vaswani et al. While models like BERT use only the encoder, many contemporary LLMs (like GPT) only employ the decoder half. Nonetheless, it's critical to comprehend the whole picture.

Encoder: Understanding and Reading

It is the encoder's responsibility to comprehend the input sequence.

- Consider the following sentence: "The cat sat on the mat." In order to capture the meanings of each word in this sentence in rich vector representations, the encoder processes each word both contextually and collectively.

The layers that each word passes through include:

- Multi-head self-attention mechanisms: These enable the model to examine every other word in the phrase in order to comprehend context. For example, the model can look at "cat" to determine who is sitting while processing the word "sat".

- Feedforward neural networks: Following attention, the signal passes through a fully connected network to refine the comprehension by introducing nonlinear changes.

- By preventing gradients from vanishing or blowing up, normalization and residual connections assist stabilize and speed up training.

Decoder: Producing the Results

The decoder takes the processed input and produces the output sequence, such as a translation or a created paragraph. Additionally, it makes use of:

- Masked self-attention: Preserves the left-to-right generation logic by preventing the model from "looking ahead" in the output sequence during training.

- Encoder-decoder attention: Allows the decoder to concentrate on pertinent segments of the input sequence while it is being generated.

The Magic in Layers

The understanding or generation is progressively refined by each encoder and decoder layer. The understanding of the model is deepened by stacking several layers, frequently dozens in today's LLMs.

2.2 Representations, Embeddings, and Tokens

Prior to being processed by a Transformer, words need to be converted into a numerical format that the model can comprehend. If we want to explain what a Transformer is really doing, we must comprehend its change.

From Text to Tokens

First, raw text is divided into tokens, which are frequently subwords rather than entire words (such as "un-," "know," and "-ing"). The model is more effective and capable of managing uncommon or complex terms thanks to this subword tokenization. Tokenizing "Understanding" into

- ['Under', '##stand', '##ing'] is one example.

After that, a defined vocabulary is used to translate each token to a distinct token ID, which is an integer.

Embeddings: Creating Vectors from IDs

After passing through an embedding layer, these token IDs become high-dimensional vectors. For example, a token ID can be transformed into a 768-dimensional vector with semantic meaning represented by floating-point values.

Each token is given a dense vector that encodes its usage and relationships based on training data in the embedding layer, which can be compared to a learnt dictionary.

Restoring Order via Positional Encoding

Transformers do not naturally comprehend the token order,

in contrast to RNNs or CNNs. This is addressed by adding positional encodings to the embeddings, which allow the model to distinguish between, for example, "the cat sat" and "sat the cat."

These encodings, which are vectors the same size as embeddings and are frequently produced using learnt embeddings or sinusoids, make sure the model is aware of each token's position in the sequence.

Hidden Representations and States

Tokens change into hidden states as they move through the Transformer's layers. The model is improving its comprehension of each token according to the context, as evidenced by these intermediate representations.

The main idea is that a token's contextualized meaning, or how the model understands a word in a given sentence, is often its final hidden state.

2.3 What Is the Real Function of Attention?

Although "attention" is the most lauded addition to Transformer models, its true purpose is frequently misinterpreted or exaggerated.

The Sense That Drives Attention

When processing a given word, attention processes enable the model to consider the significance of other words in a sequence. For example, the word "it" heavily attends to "cat" in the sentence "The cat sat on the mat because it was tired" in order to resolve the connection.

From a technical standpoint, attention calculates a score for every pair of tokens. Greater importance or influence is indicated by a higher score.

Multi-Head Focus

Transformers employ multiple heads, each with its own set of weights and learning behaviors, rather than calculating a single set of attention scores. One head may concentrate on grammatical relationships, for example.

- Another could examine long-term dependence.

- A deeper, more complex portrayal of the text is made possible by this separation.

Attention as an Explanation Myth

Attention heatmaps, which emphasize which words paid attention to others, are used as explanations in many visualizations. However, this assumption is incorrect.

Attention ≠ Explanation.

- Occasionally, importance is not correlated with high attention.
- Attention weights are not human-interpretable explanations; rather, they are model-internal mechanisms.

When Focus Is Beneficial

Even yet, attention maps can provide clues, particularly when they are obviously consistent with typical human reasoning. For instance, attention maps may demonstrate focus on the question's essential terms in activities involving responding questions.

- They may indicate which source term corresponds to a target word in translation.

However, prudence is required. It can be deceptive to rely only on attention for interpretability.

2.4 Why Size Makes Interpretability More Difficult

Small transformers are already difficult to understand. The difficulty increases exponentially at scale when using models like GPT-4 or PaLM.

The Scale Curse

There are billions of factors and hundreds of layers in modern LLMs.

- There are 175 billion parameters in GPT-3.
- GPT-4 (estimated): More than 500 billion

These parameters are dispersed among learned weights, layers, and hundreds of attention heads. It would be like attempting to track each raindrop in a storm to see how each one contributes to an output.

Emergent Behavior and Latent Concepts

Models start to display emergent behavior as they grow in size functionalities that weren't specifically programmed:

- Contextual learning
- Compositional reasoning
- Multiple-step reasoning

These skills result from the intricate relationships between millions of weights rather than from particular elements. A system that acts intelligently yet opaquely is the end result.

Scholars have discovered that latent concepts such as "sarcasm," "humor," or "justice" appear to be encoded in abstract, dispersed representations by big models. One neuron or weight alone cannot be used to comprehend them.

The Precision Illusion

Ironically, it gets harder to identify a single cause for a

model's output the more potent it is. Numerous routes through the model could result in the same output, which is one way that the complexity produces a sort of statistical haze.

- Interpretations change from being deterministic to probabilistic.

It takes more than just deciphering math or following lines on a diagram to comprehend a Transformer. It's about understanding the conceptual machinery that transforms unprocessed text into intelligent output, and then realizing how the more powerful that gear gets, the less transparent it becomes.

Understanding a model's anatomy is necessary before we can understand it:

- The process of comprehension and generation is structured by encoders and decoders.
- Human language is converted into mathematical representations through the use of tokenization and embeddings.
- Although it dynamically evaluates relationships, Attention doesn't always provide trustworthy

justifications.

- Scale presents new interpretability issues as well as new capabilities.

The question in the context of LLMs is no longer simply how does it work, but rather what does "working" even mean when a system functions at a scale or comprehension that is beyond human grasp? The tools, approaches, and frameworks needed to address it go well beyond simple model inspection. But it always starts with knowing what's going on underneath

CHAPTER 3

VISUALIZING ATTENTION: OBSERVING WHAT THE MODEL SEES

Few aspects of transformer model interpretation have captivated the interest of machine learning practitioners, engineers, and researchers as much as attention scores. These numerical indicators provide a window, albeit a hazy one, into the inner workings of complex language models by telling us how much weight a token lends to another during processing. By removing the layers of abstraction, this chapter aims to show us how attention visualization enables us to see what the model sees and, more crucially, where that vision's boundaries are.

3.1 A Comprehensive Guide to Attention Maps

Understanding what attention scores truly indicate is the first step towards comprehending attention visualization. Attention is the function in a transformer, not merely a function. As it creates context-aware representations, it decides how each token in a sequence evaluates the significance of other tokens.

Matrices and Heatmaps Across Layers and Heads

The fundamental method for calculating attention involves a dot-product mechanism between three matrices that are obtained from the token embeddings: queries, keys, and values. The attention mechanism calculates the weighted sum of all the tokens in the input sequence, including itself, for each token.

The attention matrix, which can be represented as a heatmap, is made up of these weights. In these illustrations:

- The query tokens, or the token doing the attending, are usually represented by rows.
- The key tokens, or the tokens being handled, are shown in columns.
- The heatmap's cells each show the relative importance of a query token to a key token.
- Darker hues suggest less or no attention, while brighter hues typically denote larger attention

weights.

However, attention is a distributed activity that occurs across many heads and layers. Each of the 12 layers in a common transformer, such as BERT-base, has 12 attention heads. This indicates that each input produces 144 distinct attention matrices, each of which may concentrate on distinct syntactic functions or language patterns.

What Does Each Token Address, and Why

The capacity of attention heatmaps to indicate which words "look at" which other words is one of its most intriguing features. As an illustration, consider the following sentence:

- "The cat that the dog chased was black." A head might concentrate on clarifying the relationship between "cat" and "was."
- A second head might be attracted to subject-object resolution, making a connection between "dog" and "chased."

Hovering over a token in many visualization tools shows

the entire distribution of its attention. These visualizations produce a narrative of comprehension how the model internally puts meaning together rather than merely a number map.

It is dangerous to take these maps as the absolute truth, though. Attention is not always a reliable narrator, as we shall learn later.

3.2 Trade Tools: BertViz, exBERT, and Other Resources

As transformer-based models have gained prominence, numerous tools have been created to help with attention visualization. These tools offer user-friendly interfaces for analyzing how models behave across layers, heads, and even input disturbances, in addition to streamlining the inspection process.

Configuring Your Own Workflow using Attention Visualization

One of the most popular tools for visualizing attention is

BertViz. It provides an interactive interface for investigating attention in pretrained transformer models and was created by Jesse Vig. Among its notable characteristics are:

- Navigate through each layer and attention head in the layer-wise examination process.
- Token-wise tracking: To see which other tokens a given token attends to, click on it.
- Multiple models supported: Utilizes Hugging Face's Transformers library to interface with BERT, GPT-2, RoBERTa, and other programs.

To utilize BertViz:

- Use pip to install the tool: `pip install bertviz`
- Incorporate it into a Streamlit app or Jupyter notebook.
- Utilize it with inputs that have already been processed using Hugging Face's `AutoModel` and `AutoTokenizer`.

Another effective approach, exBERT, emphasizes embedding space in addition to attentiveness. It enables users to:

- Use 2D projections to visualize token relationships.

- Examine several models using the same sentence.

- Examine the behavioral differences between various attention heads.

The following are additional cutting-edge tools:

- TensorBoard's attention plugin, which easily connects with training logs.

- The Allen Institute for AI's Ecco allows you to examine activations and model outputs in addition to attention.

How to Decipher Patterns in Various Assignments

Attention visualization's usefulness varies depending on the task:

- Key heads may concentrate on matching the query to the appropriate answer span in question-answering (QA).

- In sentiment analysis, certain heads may focus on verbs or adjectives that are emotionally charged.

- In terms of machine translation: Latent cross-lingual mappings may be revealed by using attention layers to align source and destination language tokens.

Interpretation takes on the role of a detective. You can frequently determine the "reasoning" path the model took and where it might have faltered by comparing the attention maps of accurate and inaccurate predictions.

3.3 Multi-Head Focus: Harmony Among Differences?

Transformers use multiple parallel attention heads in each layer rather than a single attention mechanism. Although they come from different projection subspaces, each head uses the same input sequence. The model can handle multiple kinds of information at once because of this approach.

The Areas of Specialization of Each Head

- Empirical research has demonstrated that attention heads specialize, defying the notion that all heads are created equal:
- Some early layer heads have a propensity to concentrate on local context (e.g., adjacent words).

- Subject-verb-object and other syntactic relationships are frequently captured by mid-layer heads.
- Subsequent minds are drawn to semantic features, such as things, themes, or even sentiment.

It's interesting to note that not all heads are created equal. Redundancy was suggested by researchers like Michel et al. (2019), who discovered that eliminating some heads had little impact on model performance.

Specialized heads, however, frequently aid in interpretability. For example, a head that regularly attends from verbs to their immediate objects can reveal dependence patterns.

- Deeper comprehension is demonstrated by a head that resolves coreference (for example, mapping "he" to "John").

How to Combine Attention While Preserving Nuance

Interpreting attention can become overwhelming because it is spread across several heads and layers. It is common practice to decrease complexity by aggregating attention scores across heads, although caution must be exercised to preserve significant differences.

- Averaging across heads is one method that is straightforward but runs the risk of hiding specialized behavior.
- Apply learnt or task-specific weights to heads according to their significance in weighted aggregate.
- The middle or last levels, which frequently include the most semantically rich signals, should be the only focus of layer-wise visualization.

The objective is to simplify the signal without oversimplifying the behavior of the model by striking a balance between clarity and fidelity.

3.4 Attention's Drawbacks as an Explanation

An increasing corpus of studies cautions against using attention maps as definitive explanations of model behavior, despite their intuitive attractiveness. The fundamental problem lies in the fact that attention is not always causally linked to the output of the model.

Pay Attention ≠ Clarification (And When It's Still Beneficial)

The fundamental conundrum is that a token's high attention does not imply that it was in charge of the output choice.

- According to studies, you may frequently change attention weights (even arbitrary ones) without having an impact on the outcome.
- It is possible to train models to generate attention maps that "look right" but are not linked to the process of reasoning.

Accordingly, attention can be descriptive rather than explanatory.

Nevertheless, attention can be useful when:
- Employed comparatively across tasks or inputs to identify patterns or irregularities.
- Additional interpretability strategies (such as gradient-based attribution and probing classifiers)

were added.

- Used when expert judgment is a component of human-in-the-loop systems.

Methods to Confirm the True Meaning of Attention

Researchers employ validation strategies like these to increase the validity of attention-based interpretations:

- Attention ablation tests: Take out tokens that need a lot of attention and see how it affects the model's predictions.
- Attention masking: To assess importance, reweight or zero out specific attention routes.
- Input perturbation tests: Modify inputs slightly to see changes in output and attention distribution.

By assisting in the triangulation of attention with causal importance, these techniques provide a more reliable image of the model's foundation.

Although not flawless, attention visualization provides an engaging glimpse into a transformer's thinking. We may start tracing the outline of model reasoning by using heatmaps, toolkits such as BertViz and exBERT, and meticulous examination of multi-head attention patterns. We must, however, approach these visualizations with a healthy dose of skepticism and enthusiasm. When utilized properly, they highlight patterns; when used improperly, they can cause confusion. They are valuable not only for what they display, but also for how effectively we comprehend what we are looking at, as is the case with all interpretive tools

CHAPTER 4

SALIENCY AND ATTRIBUTION - TRACING THE INFLUENCE OF WORDS

Modern natural language processing (NLP) models have matured into sophisticated black boxes, capable of providing impressively coherent and context-aware output. However, figuring out how these models make their decisions is still a major obstacle. Although attention processes offer one perspective on how a model functions internally, they don't always present the whole picture. This chapter delves into a potent family of strategies centered around saliency and attribution, going beyond attentiveness. By precisely tracing the impact of input words on a model's output, these techniques seek to provide a better understanding of the cause-and-effect chains found in deep NLP models.

4.1 NLP Saliency Maps

Originally a mainstay of computer vision, saliency maps show which pixels in an image have the greatest influence on a given prediction. Saliency maps, when translated to NLP, show which words or tokens have the greatest influence on the model's choice.

What Text vs. Image Saliency Means

Regions that "catch the eye" or cause the highest activation in a categorization task are frequently referred to as salient in the context of vision. This becomes more complex in text. Words have rich syntactic and semantic information, unlike pixels. Giving specific words (or tokens) significance ratings in order to indicate their increased influence on the model's output is the aim of textual saliency.

Important distinctions:

- Continuity vs. Discreteness: Text is by nature discrete, but images are continuous spatial data. A single word change can transform the meaning, while a tiny adjustment to a pixel is frequently insignificant.

- Words have a lot more abstract and compacted meaning than pixels, according to the concept of semantic density. An entire sentence's sentiment can be changed by a single word like "not."

- Sequence Dependency: Context frequently affects word influence. For instance, if "good" isn't preceded by "not," it could indicate positive sentiment.

For saliency in NLP to be effective, these intricacies must be captured.

Applying Backpropagation to Implement Saliency

Calculating the gradient of the output prediction with respect to the input embedding is one of the simplest methods for estimating saliency. This method is based on the hunch that an input component must be significant if a minor alteration results in a significant change in the output.

Procedures for creating saliency maps:

1. Forward Pass: To get the prediction (e.g., class score), pass the input through the model.

2. Compute Gradient: Calculate the gradient of the output score with respect to each input embedding.

3. Aggregation: To get a single saliency score for each token, aggregate these gradients across embedding dimensions.

4. Normalization: To enable insightful comparison and display, normalize the scores.

Despite being straightforward, this approach works well for giving a preliminary estimate of which words "mattered" in a model's forecast.

4.2 Attribution Techniques Based on Gradients

Despite providing valuable insights, simple gradient saliency maps have drawbacks such as noise and lack of robustness. To overcome these constraints, more sophisticated methods have been created, enabling more trustworthy attributions.

Guided Backpropagation and Integrated Gradients

Guided Backpropagation and Integrated Gradients (IG) are two of the most well-known methods in this field. In different ways, each enhances the raw gradient method.

Gradients (IG) that are integrated:

Developed to solve the problem of gradient saturation and local noise, IG works by computing the average gradient as the input transitions from a baseline (e.g., all-zero vector) to the real input. From the baseline to the input, the goal is to "walk" in a straight line while accumulating gradients.

Fundamental characteristics:

- Completeness: The difference between the output at the input and the baseline is equal to the sum of the attributions.
- Sensitivity: IG appropriately gives zero attribution to characteristics that do not influence the output when updated.

IG in NLP Steps:

- Select a baseline (such as a series of [PAD] or [UNK] tokens).

- Interpolate inputs between the actual input and the baseline.

- Calculate gradients at every stage.

- Multiply by the difference between the baseline and the actual input after averaging the gradients.

Backpropagation using Guidance:

This technique zeros out negative gradients during the backward pass, altering the backpropagation process. It focuses only on features that positively contribute to the decision, effectively filtering out noise.

Guided backpropagation frequently yields saliency maps that are easier to understand visually, although lacking the formal characteristics of IG.

Comparing Scores Across Layers and Tokens

By extending gradient-based techniques across layers, we may examine the network's information flow. For instance:

- Layer-wise relevance propagation: Measures how importance is passed from higher to lower layers.

- Cross-token comparisons: Indicates which tokens have an impact on the phrase both locally and internationally.

This makes it possible to comprehend attribution in three different ways: output-wise, layer-wise, and token-wise.

4.3 Influence at the Word vs. Phrase Level

While word-level attribution provides useful information, understanding language in the real world frequently relies on phrases or expressions. Attribution techniques need to be aware of interactions between multiple tokens.

Locating Important N-Grams

N-grams, or multi-word chunks, frequently have deeper meanings than the sum of their individual words. For instance, even if the word "not" is included, the sentence "not bad at all" is intrinsically positive. This would be difficult for single-token saliency unless context is modeled.

Methods to deal with this:

- Tokens belonging to the same n-gram or syntactic chunk have their attribution scores combined in a process known as "aggregated saliency."
- Dependency Parsing: Use parse trees to arrange tokens into meaningful linguistic units before allocating importance.

Better interpretability is provided by analyzing influence at this level, particularly for applications where phrases include the most important insights, such as summarization or question answering.

Sensitivity Analysis: How Much Change Breaks the Output

Sensitivity analysis is another helpful diagnostic in which input tokens are perturbed to investigate the model's output.

Two typical methods:

- Token Deletion: Take away each token individually and see how the prediction changes.
- Token Substitution: Substitute noise or synonyms for tokens and assess the effect.

High attribution is probably due to tokens or phrases that, when changed, significantly modify the outcome. By using empirical perturbations to validate the results of gradient-based approaches, this approach enhances them.

4.4 Intuitively Visualizing Impact

The way attribution is conveyed is where its real power resides. Researchers, developers, and users may all better understand model behavior by visualizing the impact of input tokens.

Influence-Based Coloring Tokens

A frequent and successful way for visualization is to color code each token based on its influence score. Tools like Captum and AllenNLP Interpret employ heatmaps over text, where warmer colors signal higher relevance.

- The following are essential guidelines for efficient visualization: Use consistent color scales for input comparison.
- In order to prevent distorting perception, it is important to properly normalize scores.
- Hovering over tokens to view their numerical attribution values is an example of how to enable interactive exploration.

Aesthetics and accuracy should be balanced in visualization to promote comprehension without changing the underlying data.

Sentiment Analysis and Summarization Case Studies

Let's examine two real-world examples where attribution and saliency strategies excel.

1. Analysis of Sentiment:

"I thought the movie would be great, but it was painfully

boring," is an example of an input sentence.

- Raw attention could draw attention to "great" and "boring."
- Saliency maps show that the negative prediction was more affected by the words "but" and "painfully."
- Integrated gradients give "painfully boring" greater weight and show the change in feeling throughout the line.

We can confirm that the model is accurately weighing contrasting conjunctions and is not being deceived by prior positive phrases thanks to this comprehensive analysis.

2. Summarization of Text:

Knowing which input segments go into the resulting summary is essential for abstractive summarization.

- Saliency maps assist in determining which words or phrases the model is concentrating on.
- Phrase-level attribution indicates if the model is maintaining its grounding in the input or

experiencing hallucinations.

- Failure scenarios can be flagged by attribution, for as when a statement that isn't important dominates the summary.

These revelations provide a way to enhance performance through data augmentation or focused retraining in addition to explaining model behavior.

A more thorough and rigorous comprehension of how language models reasoning is made possible by saliency and attribution. Attribution approaches track the true causal influence of inputs, in contrast to attention mechanisms that provide interpretability at the surface level. Combining gradients, perturbations, and visualizations gives us a comprehensive understanding of model behavior that is instructive and useful.

In the end, these resources enable researchers, developers, and even end users to transcend blind trust and create models that are not only strong but also open, responsible, and consistent with human logic

CHAPTER 5

EXPLORING THE EMBEDDING SPACE—DETERMINING VECTOR MEANING"

Much of what is considered "understanding" in the age of large-scale neural language models is concealed beneath layers of learned numerical representations. These internal spaces, also known as embedding spaces, are where unstructured language is transformed into structured information and where robots begin to understand context and subtleties. In order to gain understanding, transparency, and responsible model creation, this chapter delves deeply into the latent spaces of language models to examine how meaning is encoded, what those vectors represent, and how we might probe and analyze them.

5.1 Latent Space: What's Inside?

We start by asking the fundamental question, "What does a model actually know, and how is this knowledge stored?"

in order to comprehend embeddings.

The Development of Embeddings: From Word2Vec to Transformers

word2vec and other early language modeling techniques introduced the groundbreaking notion that words may be represented by dense vectors in a continuous space. These vectors produced significant correlations such as these after being taught by anticipating surrounding words (context):

"king" - "man" + "woman" ≈ "queen"

"Paris" - "France" + "Italy" ≈ "Rome"

We have our first genuine look at how machines might encode conceptual links thanks to this semantic arithmetic.

Transformatives like BERT, GPT, and their variants are now commonplace. These models don't just encode words but contextual tokens the vector for "bank" changes if you're talking about finance or rivers. These days, embeddings are dynamic and layer-dependent, meaning that a word's representation depends on the entire phrase in which it occurs.

Key differences include:

- Static vs. Contextualized: Transformer embeddings vary based on the sentence, whereas Word2vec embeddings are fixed upon training.
- Layered Representations: Transformers encode several kinds of information in layers, gradually constructing meaning across them.

Why "Meaning" Is Found in Hidden States

A vector is created from each token that enters a language model. We refer to these vectors as hidden states when they are modified over several levels. These stages are where the model maintains knowledge about language, not only intermediate computations.

For example, in a model trained for translation, earlier layers may learn syntactic information (e.g., part of speech), while deeper layers encode semantic roles (e.g., subject, object) and task-specific understanding (e.g., how to translate idioms). The meaning is distributed throughout these layers; they are not isolated.

This notion leads to two essential takeaways:

- The model doesn't contain a discrete symbol for "cat" or "sadness" but spreads such information across multiple integers.
- We need tools that can break down this space and reveal those hidden meanings in order to comprehend the model's conclusions.

5.2 Using t-SNE and UMAP to Visualize Embeddings

The high-dimensional space in which embeddings reside is frequently 768, 1024, or even more dimensions. Even though these spaces are rich in mathematics, humans cannot directly understand them. We project this complicated structure into 2D or 3D using dimensionality reduction techniques such as t-SNE and UMAP in order to obtain intuition.

Methods for Cutting 768 Dimensions Down to Two

Both Uniform Manifold Approximation and Projection (UMAP) and t-distributed stochastic neighbor embedding (t-SNE) are nonlinear techniques that emphasize local structure, i.e., the preservation of relationships among neighboring points.

- Although it tends to concentrate more on tight clustering, t-SNE occasionally skews the overall picture. Visualizing fine-grained categories, such as various word senses or syntactic roles, is a great use for it.
- Better preservation of global relationships is provided by UMAP, which makes it more appropriate for observing high-level trends like topic drifts or sentiment shifts.

Exposing Anomalies, Drifts, and Clusters

Upon visualizing embeddings, distinct patterns frequently surface:

- Words with similar meanings or functions, such as "happy," "joyful," and "elated," form dense clusters.

- The meaning of words like "virus" may change over time, particularly in models that are trained incrementally.
- Anomalies: Unusual token spacing or outliers may indicate data noise, adversarial training effects, or model confusion.

Positive and negative words, for example, may be found to occupy opposite regions in a sentiment classifier. However, it may indicate hidden bias if neutral words group together with a single sentiment.

Visualizing embeddings is more than academic; it's a diagnostic tool for model validation, error analysis, and even fairness auditing.

5.3 Concept Probing: Sentiment, Syntax, and Semantics

Once we've depicted meaning, the next step is to test what the model truly knows. The process of training tiny classifiers probes on top of embeddings to determine whether particular information can be recovered is known as concept probing.

Testing What Neurons "Know" with Probing Classifiers

The concept is straightforward: information must be encoded in a certain layer if a probe can determine, for example, whether a word is a noun or verb using embeddings from that layer.

Common probing tasks include:
- Sentiment Detection: Can the embeddings distinguish "love" from "hate"?
- Syntactic Roles: Can we tell which word is the subject or object?
- Grammatical Features: Does the model know gender, tense, number?

Each of these can be explored by attaching logistic regression classifiers or decision trees to specific layers and comparing accuracies.

This strategy addresses deeper questions:
- Is the model learning language principles, or merely

superficial patterns?

- At what layer does the model begin to "understand"?
- How does this differ by architecture or training data?

Does the Model Learn Grammar, Gender, or Just Word Patterns?

This distinction matters. A model that achieves high accuracy but does so by picking up spurious correlations (e.g., thinking all nurses are female) isn't learning robust language; it's increasing training bias.

Probing helps us differentiate between memorized heuristics and genuine language understanding, especially when combined with counterfactual testing (changing inputs to test model consistency).

5.4 Monitoring Embedding Drift in Fine-Tuning

Language models are rarely used "as is." Fine-tuning on a specific task (like medical question answering or legal document review) customizes the model, but it also reshapes the embedding space.

How Does Additional Training Affect Vector Space?

During fine-tuning:

- Certain embeddings become more compressed, forming tighter clusters around task-relevant categories.
- As the model reweights relevance based on the new data, other areas of the space might stretch or rotate.

While this improves performance, it can have side effects:

- Disastrous forgetting of general information.
- In the event that the fine-tuning data is skewed, bias reinforcement will be applied.
- Loss of interpretability due to the distortion of formerly significant directions in the space.

Detecting Bias Shifts and Overfitting

One useful technique to monitor these changes is to compare embeddings before and after fine-tuning using distance metrics (e.g., cosine similarity). While fluctuations along social or identity dimensions may indicate bias amplification, significant drift in high-variance directions may indicate overfitting.

- For instance, it is a warning sign if, after fine-tuning on certain clinical texts, the embedding of "doctor" approaches "male."
- Overconfidence may be indicated if "uncertain" terms, such as "maybe" or "perhaps," change dramatically in a classifier.

An early warning system for identifying instability, ethical risks, or task misalignment in model development is embedded drift analysis.

Anyone who wants to create, improve, or implement language models responsibly must have a solid understanding of what occurs in the embedding space. These spaces are not merely mathematical artifacts they constitute the actual medium through which models "think." When we probe, examine, and monitor these vectors, we open a new level of interpretability that bridges the gap between machine learning and human intuition.

Through this lens, we stop perceiving models as black boxes and begin treating them as systems of learned relationships, capable of insight, but also prone to misinterpretation. Therefore, it is our responsibility to move through this area with diligence, clarity, and a dedication to openness

CHAPTER 6

FROM SHAP TO LIME INTRODUCING CONVENTIONAL XAI TOOLS INTO THE WORLD OF LARGE LANGUAGE MODELS

One pattern emerges from the ongoing development of machine learning models: larger, more complex architectures, such as foundation models and converters, predominate. On a variety of tasks, these models which include BERT, GPT, and their variations have demonstrated exceptional performance. However, transparency suffers as a result of this power. The question, "Why did the model make this decision?" frequently lingers with users, stakeholders, and even engineers.

To overcome this opacity, Explainable AI (XAI) provides a collection of resources and techniques. Particularly well-known for providing clear, useful insights into black-box models are model-agnostic tools such as SHAP (SHapley Additive exPlanations) and LIME (Local Interpretable Model-Agnostic Explanations). However, there are distinct opportunities and challenges when modifying these tools for Natural Language Processing (NLP), particularly for large language models (LLMs). This chapter examines the mechanics, real-world modifications, hybrid innovations, and trade-offs of these traditional XAI techniques in order to determine how they might be modified for NLP.

6.1 The Concept of Shapley Values for Words and How SHAP Operates in NLP

Cooperative game theory is the foundation of SHAP. In NLP, every feature (or word) is viewed as a "player" in a game, with the model's output serving as the "payout." The average marginal contribution of a word to the prediction across all potential word subsets is measured by the Shapley value.

Using Text Data with SHAP

Every token, usually a word or subword unit contributes to the final prediction in natural language processing. By methodically comparing the effects of each token's presence against absence in the input, SHAP calculates the impact of each token. However, tabular data is more straightforward than text.

Important textual adaptations include:

- Tokenization Sensitivity: The tokenization of the text has a significant impact on SHAP explanations. A single word may be divided into several tokens, each of which receives a distinct SHAP value, utilizing models such as GPT using Byte-Pair Encoding (BPE) or BERT using WordPiece.

- Contextual Embeddings: LLMs compute embeddings contextually, in contrast to traditional models. A word's significance can change based on its surrounding words. SHAP needs to be modified to take this dynamic into account.

Baseline Inputs: A feature's "missing" value must be defined by SHAP. This could be a gray pixel in an image or a mean or null in tabular data. The definition of "missing" in NLP is a complex concept. Typical tactics consist of:

- Masking the word (if [MASK] tokens are supported by the model)
- Substituting a neutral token or UNK for the term
- Deleting the term entirely

Model-Agnostic Explanation of Token Importance

SHAP can deal with any black-box model by considering it as a function that accepts input and returns output. Because of its model-agnostic nature, SHAP is both computationally costly and adaptable.

When used with NLP, SHAP provides:

- The token-level contribution is represented by color-coded heatmaps, where positive and negative influences on the prediction are indicated by red and green highlights, respectively.
- Insights at the phrase level: Classifying token values can provide insights at the named entity, noun phrase, or sentiment phrase level.

For instance, in mood classification: > "The film was painfully long and incredibly dull."

SHAP might show:

- "incredibly" and "dull" have substantial negative contributions
- "painfully" improves the negative classification

- "long" might contribute mildly or neutrally depending on context

These values offer a granular perspective into what the model really saw as decisive.

6.2 LIME for Language Models How Perturbation-Based Explanations Help in Local Contexts

LIME works differently than SHAP. To approximate the behavior of the complicated model close to a particular instance, LIME constructs a local surrogate model rather than analyzing every potential subset of features. This local approximation is generally linear, offering an intuitive notion of feature relevance around the neighborhood of the data point.

Text Explanations with LIME

In NLP, LIME randomly removes or replaces words to produce perturbed versions of the input text, then examines how the predictions change. LIME can determine which words are most crucial by looking at which word removals have the biggest impact on the forecast.

For instance: "The performance was inspiring and breathtaking," was the original statement.

LIME might produce the following:

- "The performance was inspiring." Prediction declines by 20%
- "The performance was stunning and amazing." Prediction declines by 15%
- "It was amazing and motivating." $\rightarrow$ 30% decrease in prediction

LIME deduces from these variances that "performance," "breathtaking," and "inspiring" have a significant impact.

Benefits in Regional Settings

The local focus of LIME is its strength:

- Faithfulness in limited scope: LIME's local linear model provides a faithful snapshot of decision limits close to the instance, even in cases when the global model is complex and non-linear.
- Interpretability: Word significance is immediately

shown by the coefficients in the local model.

- Adaptability: LIME may be used with any output, including classification, regression, and even probability scores, and is independent of model architecture.

Applying LIME to Transformer-based models such as BERT, GPT, and others presents particular difficulties:

- Contextualized Predictions: A single word change can significantly alter the sentence's meaning. Cascade effects must be taken into consideration by LIME.

- Embedding Disruptions: The surrogate model may be distorted by perturbations that result in Out-of-Vocabulary tokens or embeddings that don't represent natural language.

Mitigation techniques:

- Limit disruptions to removing words only, not replacing them.

- Make use of synonyms or semantically equivalent substitutes.

- Use a language model to filter out non-fluent disturbances

The perturbation method used by LIME can be very useful for intent identification, toxicity detection, and text classification. LIME, for instance, can assist in ensuring that irrelevant cues, such as usernames or greetings, do not bias the model in customer support chatbots.

6.3 Hybrid Methods: Harmonizing Native and External Interpretability Attention + SHAP

Internal interpretability cues, such as attention weights, are already available in modern language models. When processing each token, the model's attention mechanisms determine how much emphasis is placed on various input components.

However, attention is not a complete explanation method:

- Attention does not always correlate with feature relevance.
- Although they may receive a lot of attention, some layers may not add much to the final product.

A hybrid approach that combines attention (an internal mechanism) and SHAP (external XAI) can provide more complex and trustworthy explanations.

Why Combine Techniques for Interpretability?

- Simply paying attention is not enough: It provides salience but not contribution.
- SHAP by itself is computationally costly: It is possible to limit the focus by adding attention priors.
- Multifaceted hybrid insights: One draws attention, the other has an effect.

Building Richer Explanations with Multiple Lenses

A strong explanation pipeline could resemble this:

1. Extract attention scores from several layers of the transformer.
2. To assess word-level contribution, Run SHAP.
3. Purple and black:
4. High-SHAP and high-attention words: Essential
5. High SHAP but poor focus: Dependencies that are hidden
6. Attention-grabbing yet low SHAP: Potentially deceptive emphasis

This enables professionals to:

- More accurately diagnose model behavior - Find any erroneous associations
- Verify whether the model's emphasis is in line with domain expertise.

This layered interpretability helps guarantee that conclusions are based on pertinent evidence, not artifacts, in delicate applications like medical record summarization or legal document classification.

6.4 Interpretability vs Performance Trade-off *SHAP/LIME Computation Cost in LLMs

Despite their might, SHAP and LIME are not free. Significant computational cost is introduced when using these techniques on LLMs.

Why Do NLP Tools Like SHAP and LIME Cost So Much?

Sentences containing dozens or hundreds of tokens are considered high-dimensional inputs.

- Model complexity: GPT-3 has billions of parameters, whereas BERT-base has 110 million.

- All feature combinations are approximated by SHAP: Number of evaluations complexity that is exponential

- For every explanation, LIME produces hundreds of perturbations.

For large-scale deployments, running explanations on a single instance is impracticable because it can take several seconds to minutes.

When to Apply Full-Scale vs. Lightweight Analysis

Knowing the use case aids in figuring out how much explanation is required:

When: The decision has high stakes (e.g., healthcare, legal, finance), use full-scale analysis (SHAP or LIME).

- Post-hoc validation of the model's bias or fairness is required.

- The behavior of the model is being audited or reviewed by the government.

When: Requires real-time interpretability (e.g., live chatbot explanations), use lightweight alternatives.

- A fast diagnostic is required, such as debugging model predictions.
- Millions of inferences are made every day, so you're working at scale.

The following are examples of lightweight options:

Attention heatmaps

- Integrated gradients, which are less costly than SHAP
- Models based on prototypes with illustrative examples

Particularly in the age of LLMs, the use of SHAP and LIME in NLP goes beyond simple porting. It calls for careful adaptation, rigorous engineering, and careful interpretation. When properly applied, these techniques can shed light on the cryptic logic of strong language models, fostering confidence in AI systems among developers, users, and stakeholders.

By combining traditional XAI methods with the

requirements of contemporary NLP, we produce explanations that are both comprehensible to humans and mathematically sound. By doing this, we bridge the gap between human understanding and model prediction, transforming AI into more than just intelligent but also responsible

CHAPTER 7

IDENTIFYING AND EXPLAINING MODEL PREJUDICE
DIAGNOSING BIAS

Fairness, inclusivity, and ethical responsibility are just as important as excellent performance or linguistic fluency in the field of artificial intelligence, particularly when working with large language models (LLMs). The possible harm from embedded biases becomes a pressing problem as these models become more prevalent in digital assistants, decision-making systems, education, hiring, and law enforcement. This chapter delves further into the comprehension, detection, and interpretation of bias in LLMs and provides helpful advice on how to use explainability techniques to reveal and lessen prejudice in AI systems.

7.1 The Signs of Bias in LLMs

Bias in AI is not only a theoretical topic. It shows up as

outputs that, frequently without giving users any prior notice, reflect, amplify, or distort systemic imbalances. By definition, language models are influenced by the data they use. The internet, which represents both the beauty and the brokenness of human civilization, is a source of knowledge for them.

Types of Bias Frequently Seen:

- Gender Bias: Many LLMs are more likely to respond with "he" when asked, "The doctor said," while "The nurse said" frequently results in "she." Traditional gender roles are reflected in and reinforced by these biases.

- Ethnic and Racial Bias: Certain ethnic names may be unjustly connected to poverty, criminality, or unfavorable stereotypes. For example, compared to prompts that use "White man," "Black man was stopped by police because…" frequently elicit harsher or more criminalized completions.

- Bias in Politics and Ideology: LLMs may lean liberal

or conservative, depending on the data source and fine-tuning technique. Indicating ideological asymmetry, questions like "Why is capitalism bad?" could elicit more critical responses than "Why is socialism bad?"

The Reason This Occurs:

- Learning driven by data: Massive corpora, including books, news stories, Wikipedia entries, Reddit conversations, and Twitter messages, are used to train LLMs. Both overt and covert biases are frequently present in these sources.

- The use of statistical mimicry The purpose of LLMs is to forecast the next most likely word or phrase. The model learns and replicates biases if they are statistically prevalent in the data.

- Effects of Amplification: Due to biased user feedback or reinforcement loops, these models have the potential to magnify the patterns already present in the data once they have been refined or implemented in particular applications.

Bias is not always harmful. The statistical fabric of our environment is the source of this emergent phenomenon. However, acknowledging this does not excuse us from dealing with it.

7.2 Examining Results for Prejudice

We must be able to recognize bias before we can mitigate it. By using interpretability tools, we may examine black-box models and identify the ways and locations in which bias enters the system. The methods for identifying biased behavior in LLM outputs are examined in this section.

Case Studies: Prejudicial Outcomes

Let's look at a few example situations:

"The engineer explained the solution because she was," is the prompt.

"...emotional about her work" is the completion.

- Analysis: The model may implicitly identify women with emotional thinking rather than technical expertise.

Prompt: "Jamal, the suspect, was captured after.

"A violent confrontation with the police" is the final phrase.

Prompt (Control): "Greg, the suspect, was captured after..."

"...a misunderstanding at the store" is the conclusion.

- Analysis: Negative, violent occurrences are more frequently associated with names that are stereotypically associated with Black people.

One way to assess these cases is by using:

Visualization of Attention: It is possible to determine which aspects of the input prompt have a disproportionate impact on the output by looking at where the model concentrates its attention. The weighting of names, pronouns, or important terms during prediction can be monitored with the use of tools such as BertViz.

- Mapping of Token Importance: One can determine whether particular gender or racial tokens elicit biased responses by ranking tokens according to their impact on the final output using Integrated Gradients or SHAP (SHapley Additive exPlanations).

- The process of embedding clusters The spatial arrangement of various identities can be seen by analyzing the vector space of model embeddings. Closer clusters, such as "criminal" and "Black," can suggest linkage or conflation.

Visual Aids for Exposing Bias:

Attention head heatmaps can reveal whether identity words (such as "woman") are regularly highlighted more negatively across a range of outputs.

- Counterfactual gradients: Show how minor adjustments (such as substituting "she" for "he") affect the probability of specific completions.

- An essential first step in achieving accountability is exposing bias. We cannot trust something we do not comprehend if we do not interpret it.

7.3 Data Interventions and Counterfactual Testing

We must use systematic testing frameworks and move beyond anecdotal triggers in order to thoroughly evaluate model behavior for bias. A potent technique is counterfactual testing, which entails carefully altering inputs to see how outputs differ.

Gender and Name Swapping:

Changing identity-related terms while maintaining all other terms is a traditional technique for evaluating bias.

Original Prompt: "John leads very well. He constantly takes the initiative.
The following is a counterfactual prompt: "Mary is a great leader." She is always the one to take charge.

Disparities can be brought to light by comparing the completions or confidence scores. Bias is present if Mary's version results in follow-ups that are less authoritative or more emotionally charged.

You may scale this using:

- Generation of Templates: Use templates that contain names from various racial, gender, and religious backgrounds to automate prompt production.

- A/B Prompt Scale Testing: Use statistical techniques to examine thousands of prompt-completion pairings in order to assess bias patterns.

Comparing Embedding Spaces:

- A hidden window into the model's mental grasp of language is provided by embeddings. Here are some methods for detecting bias:

- This test, known as the Direct Bias Test" (Bolukbasi

et al., 2016), determines whether a characteristic (such "doctor") is more closely associated with one gender than the other in embedding space.

- The Word Embedding Association Test, or WEAT, is: measures how target concepts (like male or female) and qualities (like career or family) are related.

- By sampling hidden layers, these tools which were initially created for static word embeddings are modified for dynamic contextual embeddings in LLMs.

Information-Based Interventions

Correcting a prejudice that has been verified entails:

- Data Augmentation: During training, provide additional counter-stereotypical or balanced samples.

- Reweighting: During fine-tuning, modify loss functions to penalize biased outputs.

- Data Filtering: Eliminate or mark training set examples that reinforce negative stereotypes.

Not all bias is a bad thing. It can occasionally be a mirror. However, we are able to regulate the reflection by conducting rigorous counterfactual testing.

7.4 Explainability as an Instrument for Equity

Explainability is an ethical tool as well as a diagnostic tool. When applied appropriately, explainable AI (XAI) promotes accountability in practical applications, facilitates transparency, and supports fairness audits.

Debiasing Techniques Guided by XAI:

- Post-Hoc Analysis: To find consistently skewed patterns, apply attention analysis, SHAP, or LIME following model inference.

- Proactive Fine-Tuning: Iteratively correct biased tendencies by training on bias-exposed datasets and monitoring XAI results.

- Multi-Lens Assessment: To determine where and how bias occurs, combine several explanation types, such as gradient-based attributions, perturbation analysis, and attention scores.

Examples of Use in Various Industries:

- Content Moderation: To ensure that no community is unfairly singled out, XAI can assist human reviewers in comprehending why a model highlighted or failed to flag particular content.

- Hiring Algorithms: When used in conjunction with LIME or SHAP, tools such as Fairlearn can show whether an LLM-based resume screener penalizes applicants based on their names, genders, or universities.

- Legal Risk Assessment: In the legal field, transparency in automated decision-making systems is essential. Algorithmic conclusions are increasingly being required by courts to be explicable. XAI makes it possible to adhere to regulatory requirements for equity and openness.

Performance and Interpretability in Balance:

There is frequently conflict between creating completely interpretable models and models that function well. Despite their potency, large models are opaque. Smaller models may perform worse, but they are crisper. By enabling stakeholders to have faith in big models without sacrificing insight, XAI helps close this gap.

Things to Think About:

- Interpretability tools can occasionally be overly complicated or deceptive.
- Some biases are contextual and subtle, making them difficult to quantify.
- Resolving model bias alone won't solve the fundamental inequities in society data.

However, adopting explainability raises AI above simple

computing to cognition that is comparable to that of humans.

In large language models, identifying and fixing bias is a duty, not an optional feature. The integrity of these models' outputs must be above reproach as they are integrated into systems that influence people's lives and society. The biases that would otherwise remain hidden beneath the surface can be exposed, examined, and subdued with the use of tools like SHAP, LIME, embedding analyses, and counterfactual testing.

Explainability serves as our guiding light in the dark. It enables us to understand not just what models say, but also the reasons behind it. By doing this, we are addressing the social algorithms that exist within us and creating models that respect the human narratives that underlie language in addition to debugging code

CHAPTER 8

DEBUGGING HALLUCINATIONS—WHEN MODELS INVENT THINGS

One phenomenon that stands out as a challenge and a risk as artificial intelligence continues to permeate sectors and applications is hallucinations. Hallucinations in the context of large language models (LLMs) are the creation of information that appears to be true but is completely false. Hallucinations can undermine confidence in AI systems by misattributing quotes, fabricating studies that don't exist, or presenting facts that are blatantly false.

This chapter will examine the characteristics of hallucinations in LLMs, explain why they happen even in extremely complex models, and go over methods for identifying and preventing them. In conclusion, you'll have useful tools and methods for figuring out when your model is "making things up" and how to make sure its outputs are accurate.

8.1 In LLMs, what is a hallucination?

Fundamentally, a language model hallucination occurs when the system produces information that is erroneous, impossible to verify, or nonsensical, but nevertheless seems reasonable to a human observer. From falsified citations and incorrect quotes to outright fraudulent claims regarding historical events or scientific evidence, hallucinations can take many different shapes. In fields where accuracy is crucial, such as healthcare, the legal system, and finance, these hallucinations can be very harmful.

The following are typical types of hallucinations in LLMs:

- Fake Citations: A model may boldly cite a study, book, or journal article that doesn't exist, like "As cited in Journal of Advanced Neuroscience 2019, page 33...." It can be challenging to identify this fake citation, particularly if it is accompanied by data that seem plausible, such as precise dates or page numbers.

- Inaccurate Quotations: Quotations produced by models may seem realistic, yet they may be erroneous or completely fabricated. For example, when a quote never existed, it can ascribe it to a famous person like Albert Einstein.

- Self-Assured Silence: LLMs may generate remarks that sound confident but are factually inaccurate. A model might state, for example, that "the Earth orbits the Sun in 220 days," which might seem authoritative from a scientific standpoint yet be essentially incorrect.

The Reason It Occurs Even in "Smart" Models

Because LLMs are inherently probabilistic, hallucinations occur. These models use patterns in the data they have been trained on to anticipate the most likely word sequence rather than comprehending facts the way people do. This occurs for the following reasons:

- Pattern Matching, Incomprehension: Although

LLMs are quite good at identifying patterns and anticipating the subsequent word in a series, they are not able to "understand" the world in the same way that humans do. A model may learn that citing a study or citation is frequently a good method to appear credible even if the research doesn't exist if it has read a lot of material that mentions scientific studies.

- The lack of ground truth: Other than their training data, LLMs are not able to access real-time data from validated sources. Due to this restriction, they are able to produce content that is out-of-date or just incorrect because they lack an internal system for fact-checking.

- Complexity of Representing Knowledge: Because it is enmeshed in high-dimensional regions, the model's knowledge might not accurately capture the complexities of reality. As a result, while producing answers, it could mix disparate facts in ways that seem reasonable at first glance but are in fact erroneous or internally inconsistent.

The first step to reducing hallucinations is to understand why they happen. Learning to recognize them when they show up in outputs, however, is the next obstacle.

8.2 Fact Tracing Attribution Maps

Tracing the information flow in the model is one of the best methods for comprehending and debugging hallucinations in LLMs. An effective technique for visualizing how a model arrives at a specific result is an attribution map, which shows which sources and tokens helped produce potentially inaccurate data.

Showing Generated Claims' Source Tokens

Attribution maps assist in highlighting the tokens that a model most frequently used to produce a given assertion. You may determine whether the model is using accurate sources or creating details by mapping the words it concentrated on during the generating phase.

For instance, the attribution map may reveal that an LLM

predicated a fake quote it created and credited to a well-known scientist on a number of irrelevant information or data pieces, leading to an irrational conclusion. Finding this pattern is essential to comprehending how a model could experience hallucinations in a specific situation.

Knowledge Flow Mapping in Multi-Turn Prompts

For LLMs, multi-turn discussions are especially challenging because the model needs to preserve context throughout several exchanges. Attribution maps become even more crucial in these situations for illustrating the information flow between turns. Attribution maps can assist in determining whether the model is misinterpreting prior comments or conflating context from earlier turns if a hallucination follows multiple exchanges.

In certain instances, a sequence of minor errors that build up over time may cause the hallucination rather than the rapid reaction. You can more successfully fix any weak places in the model's reasoning process by examining how tokens move across multi-turn prompts.

8.3 Methods of Intervention

Intervention is the next step when hallucinations are identified. Reducing or stopping the production of inaccurate or fraudulent information is the aim. Models can be guided toward more dependable results using a variety of strategies.

Guiding Corrections with Attention and Saliency

Modern LLMs process and generate language mostly through attention mechanisms. We may gain a better understanding of the aspects of the input the model is concentrating on while producing a response by utilizing attention maps. Examining the attention map might reveal whether a model is excessively focused on unimportant or untrustworthy aspects of the input if it generates a hallucinated truth.

Maps of saliency: These maps emphasize how crucial each token or attribute in the input is to achieving a specific result. We may urge the model to concentrate on more reliable, pertinent information and lessen its dependence on potentially deceptive cues by modifying the saliency distribution.

The use of attention shaping for bias correction: The model can be explicitly directed away from regions where hallucinations are most likely to occur by altering the attention allocation during inference. This could entail focusing on factual content or diverting attention from unrelated sources.

Using Ground-Truth and Retrieval to Anchor Models

Models must be based on validated facts in order to reduce hallucinations. Among the most effective methods for this is retrieval-augmented generation (RAG). The model in this configuration does not produce content only from its internal training data. Rather, before producing a response, it gathers pertinent facts from a well curated knowledge base, including scholarly publications, databases, or reliable websites.

RAG stands for retrieval-augmented generation. RAG

helps guarantee that the generated material is grounded in factual information by anchoring the model in external, validated sources. The likelihood of hallucinations is significantly decreased because the model must retrieve supporting information when it attempts to generate a fact.

Retrieval based on embedding: By using embedding-based retrieval, models can incorporate contextually relevant information instead of depending on conventional search engines. We may better regulate the information flow and lessen the possibility of hallucinated facts by including these retrieval methods into the architecture of the model.

When used properly, these intervention strategies can dramatically lower the frequency and intensity of hallucinations, enhancing the dependability of models.

8.4 Knowing When to Believe the Model: A Heuristic Based on Visuals

There will always be situations where exercising caution is necessary to trust a model's output, even with the most sophisticated intervention approaches. To assist human operators in determining when to trust a model, we can provide dashboards and visual heuristics that highlight possible hallucinations.

Creating Hallucination Detection Dashboards

For identifying patterns in hallucinations, dashboards that monitor model performance over time might be quite helpful. These dashboards can offer real-time insights about the parts of the model's behavior that are most vulnerable to fabrications by continuously examining the model's outputs.

Instant Feedback: Real-time feedback regarding the dependability of a model's output, including confidence scores, source reliability, and a "hallucination likelihood" indicator, should be provided by these dashboards. This statistic could be produced by identifying departures from expected behavioral patterns or by comparing the model's output against validated data.

Verification by Humans in the Loop: Although a model might offer a solution, the dashboard might ask a human operator to confirm the veracity of some statements prior to their publication or implementation. By taking a "human-in-the-loop" approach, hallucinations are detected before they do damage.

Transparency-focused prompt engineering

Prompt engineering is also essential for preventing hallucinations. You can lessen the possibility that the model will produce false information by creating prompts that direct it toward accurate data.

Transparent Prompts: Create prompts like "Based on your knowledge, provide a summary of the key studies supporting this statement" that urge the model to be open and honest about its rationale. The model is encouraged to source its answers more carefully by this kind of challenge.

The following are fact-checking prompts: Asking the model directly to confirm the facts it produces is another method. "Can you provide a citation for that claim?" is one example. This straightforward exercise can lessen hallucinations by making the model recognize when there is insufficient evidence to sustain them.

One of the most difficult problems that huge language models are now dealing with is hallucinations. As we've seen, these fabrications result from the probabilistic nature of these models, which are excellent at identifying patterns but are prone to "making things up" when they don't have enough context or trustworthy data. We can reduce hallucinations and create more reliable AI systems by utilizing visual heuristics, attribution maps, and intervention strategies. Nevertheless, human operators still bear the ultimate duty for ensuring that the model's output is accurate, dependable, and morally sound, even with these tools in place. Knowing whether to trust a model is just as important as knowing how it produces its outputs in a future where artificial intelligence (AI) technologies are increasingly used in decision-making

CHAPTER 9

EXPLAINABILITY FOR REGULATORY COMPLIANCE

As AI develops further, its incorporation into a variety of industries has emerged as a key component of the technological environment. But as AI becomes more potent, there is also a greater need for accountability and transparency. In many jurisdictions, AI is now subject to a developing set of laws that demands explainability. The importance of explainability in regulatory compliance is examined in this chapter, especially as governments and organizations worldwide implement regulations to guarantee that AI systems are open, equitable, and intelligible to all parties involved.

This chapter's main goal is to walk readers through the explainability notion, why it's important for regulatory compliance, and how businesses may use interpretability strategies to satisfy ethical and legal requirements while simultaneously utilizing transparency as a competitive advantage.

9.1 International AI Transparency Regulations

The global movement to regulate AI in recent years has produced a number of extensive frameworks designed to guarantee that AI systems continue to be transparent, safe, and equitable. In order to increase the understandability and accountability of AI choices, these policies usually place a strong emphasis on explainability. Let's examine the main laws influencing this environment.

The Right to Explanation under the GDPR

One of the most important pieces of law governing privacy and data protection in the European Union is the General Data Protection Regulation (GDPR). The right to explanation is one of its most important clauses in relation to AI. Article 22 of the GDPR states that, absent certain circumstances, people shouldn't be the subject of decisions made exclusively on the basis of automated processing, including profiling. One of these requirements is that people have the right to an explanation when automated systems make decisions for them.

The GDPR's right to explanation basically states that if a decision made by an AI system affects a person, they have a right to know how and why that decision was reached. This right is essential for promoting accountability and transparency in AI systems by guaranteeing that people can question and challenge judgments that might be unfair or discriminating.

The EU AI Act: Controlling AI at High Risk

The EU AI Act, a comprehensive law that categorizes AI systems according to their danger levels, is another project that the European Union is currently working on. Strict regulations apply to high-risk AI systems, which include AI utilized in fields including healthcare, criminal justice, and finance. The principles of explainability and transparency are fundamental requirements for high-risk AI systems. Organizations are required by the EU AI Act to give concise justifications for the decisions made by AI systems, particularly when such decisions have a substantial influence on people's lives.

Because the EU AI Act places a strong emphasis on transparency, developers must make sure that even non-experts can easily audit and understand their AI systems. This entails giving precise explanations of the training process, prediction processes, and data sources used by the models. In order for stakeholders to evaluate the efficacy and fairness of AI systems, this rule also mandates continuous monitoring and the production of easily accessible reports.

Regulatory Frameworks in the United States: Ethical AI Principles and Beyond"

Although AI regulations are less centralized in the US, there is still a rising emphasis on AI responsibility and transparency. Guidelines for AI openness have been released by a number of government organizations, including the government Trade Commission (FTC). Furthermore, a number of U.S. states have put their own laws governing AI into effect, especially when it comes to hiring and credit scoring.

Although there isn't a complete national AI regulation like the EU AI Act, U.S. regulators are pushing businesses to incorporate explainability into their AI systems as a fundamental component and are focusing more on ethical AI practices. The U.S. The Department of Commerce, for example, has established guidelines for trustworthy AI that stress the need of AI being transparent and intelligible, particularly when it comes to high-stakes decision-making.

The True Meaning of the "Right to Explanation"

AI models and systems are required by law to provide stakeholders, especially those affected by automated decisions, with an explanation of their decision-making process. This is known as the right to explanation. This implies that companies must make sure their AI models are interpretable, which means that the typical user or stakeholder can understand the logic behind a decision. The right to explanation guarantees that AI systems continue to be held accountable, whether that means giving a brief explanation of the reasoning behind a specific proposal or a more thorough analysis of the contributing elements.

9.2 Interpretability in Documentation

Effective interpretability procedures not only satisfy legal requirements but also assist businesses in preserving confidence, provide insight into model behavior, and guarantee that systems operate as intended. A strong approach to documentation through interpretability is essential for firms looking to maintain regulatory compliance.

Audits Using Visualization and Probes

Visualization is one of the best methods to guarantee transparency in AI systems. Developers and auditors can see how a model prioritizes and analyzes input information to produce its outputs by using visual tools like heat maps, saliency maps, and attention maps. Organizations can more readily identify biases, mistakes, or inconsistencies in their models by visualizing the decision-making process. This might be crucial for preserving regulatory compliance.

Maps of saliency: These maps show which aspects of the

input data have the greatest bearing on the model's judgment. To help doctors better understand the reasoning behind a suggestion, a saliency map might, for instance, display which features of an image influenced the model's diagnosis in a medical diagnostic model.

Maps of Attention: These maps show the contributions of various input tokens (words, phrases, or attributes) to the model's predictions, which can assist explain why particular choices are taken and whether they produce the desired results.

Building Reports on Interpretability with Examples

A critical challenge for AI systems that must adhere to rules is producing comprehensive interpretability reports. In addition to outlining the decision-making process, these reports ought to provide instances of actual decision-making procedures, preferably with data that closely resembles the inputs the model would really encounter during deployment.

An interpretability report for a credit scoring AI, for

example, might give a summary of the model's decision-making process, illustrate how various elements (such as income, debt, and credit history) affect the final score, and give examples of when the model evaluated a credit application correctly and incorrectly.

For regulators, auditors, and other stakeholders who need to confirm that the model functions as intended and complies with legal and ethical requirements, these reports are quite helpful. It is simpler for firms to prove compliance during audits or inspections when they have such reports available.

9.3 Case Studies from the Real World

Let's examine a few real-world instances where AI transparency is crucial to regulatory compliance in order to better appreciate the significance of explainability in practice.

Model Diagnosis Explanations in Healthcare

AI is being used more and more in healthcare for

diagnoses, but because medical decision-making carries such high stakes, it is important to understand how these systems make their decisions. An AI model that evaluates medical images, like MRIs or X-rays, for example, needs to be able to justify its identification of a certain image as having symptoms of an illness, like cancer.

Explainability enters the picture here. Healthcare professionals must have confidence that the AI's suggestions are supported by clear, reasonable logic. For instance, if an AI system suggests that a patient undergo more testing, both physicians and patients need to be able to comprehend the rationale behind the advice. Regulatory agencies could demand thorough justifications of the characteristics the model used to diagnose the patient, such as particular abnormalities found in the medical imaging or the existence of particular biomarkers.

Finance: Transformer-Based Explainable Credit Scoring

AI is frequently used in the finance industry for credit scoring, which establishes a person's or company's eligibility for loans or other financial services. Regulators, however, may have serious concerns about the opaqueness of some AI models, particularly deep learning models like transformers, particularly when it comes to discrimination and justice.

Financial firms can now give transparent and intelligible justifications for credit decisions thanks to explainable AI in credit scoring models. When an AI model rejects a loan application, for instance, the lender can reveal to the applicant which factors—like income, credit history, or debt-to-income ratio—were most important in making the decision.

Financial institutions can adhere to regulations and exhibit fairness by employing interpretable models or post-hoc explanation techniques, such as SHAP values (Shapley additive explanations) or LIME (local interpretable model-agnostic explanations). This ensures that applicants comprehend the rationale behind decisions and have the opportunity to challenge or appeal decisions that may be viewed as unjust.

9.4 The Competitive Advantage of Explainability

Explainability can provide a substantial competitive advantage in the marketplace, even though regulatory rules must be followed. Businesses may differentiate their goods in an increasingly crowded AI market and forge closer bonds with regulators, investors, and consumers by putting a high priority on openness.

Building Trust With Users Through Openness

Adoption of AI-driven solutions depends heavily on trust, particularly in delicate industries like healthcare, banking, and law enforcement. Businesses can gain the trust of users who might otherwise have doubts about the dependability and equity of AI systems by offering clear explanations of how these systems make their choices. Users are more inclined to follow recommendations and have faith in the technology when they comprehend the reasoning behind the model's suggestions.

Using Visibility to Set Your AI Product Apart

Businesses that place a high priority on explainability can set themselves apart from rivals in today's cutthroat market by demonstrating their dedication to accountability and openness. Making your AI system's decision-making process transparent to clients whether via interactive visualizations, clear reports, or thorough model documentation can help you differentiate yourself from rivals who depend on opaque, "black-box" technologies.

Additionally, businesses who proactively implement explainability policies will be better equipped to adjust to changing regulations and minimize the risk of non-compliance, which can result in expensive fines or harm to their brand as regulatory frameworks get harsher.

Explainability is becoming a crucial element of safety, trust, and compliance in the constantly changing field of AI legislation. Demands for transparency in AI decision-making are rising, thanks to both particular U.S. governmental initiatives and international frameworks like the EU AI Act and GDPR. In addition to adhering to legislation, companies that value explainability and embrace interpretability in their AI systems will forge closer bonds with stakeholders, users, and regulators. Organizations can transform explainability from a legal necessity into a competitive advantage and establish themselves as pioneers in the moral application of AI technology by making investments in thorough documentation, visualization strategies, and real-world case studies

CHAPTER 10

BUILDING THE INTERPRETABILITY TOOLKIT

Achieving explainability and interpretability is becoming more and more important in the quickly developing field of artificial intelligence, especially in the area of large language models (LLMs). Although strong AI models like deep neural networks and transformers provide performance never seen before, their opaqueness can cause problems with ethics, compliance, and trust. The goal of this chapter is to compile the methods and tools required to improve the transparency and understandability of AI systems, particularly LLMs. In order to make complicated AI systems more understandable for developers, stakeholders, and end users, we'll look at how to create an interpretability toolkit that combines a number of methods and technologies.

Interpretability is now a necessary component of AI development rather than a luxury or optional extra, particularly for applications that have a direct impact on people's lives like healthcare, banking, and law enforcement. In order to demystify complex AI models, let's explore the processes required to create a strong interpretability pipeline that integrates tools, methodologies, and workflows.

10.1 Creating Your LLM XAI Pipeline

In order to comprehend and convey the decision-making process of big language models, it is necessary to combine several interpretability techniques while creating an efficient explainable AI (XAI) pipeline. Because of their intricate designs and large number of parameters, LLMs may seem like mysterious systems. Transparency must therefore be incorporated into all stages of development by AI practitioners in order to foster trust and guarantee regulatory compliance.

Combining Tools: Saliency, SHAP, and Attention

Several tools and techniques should be integrated to provide a thorough understanding of how the model processes inputs and produces outputs in order to build a strong XAI pipeline for LLMs.

- Attention Mechanisms: In LLMs, particularly in transformers, attention mechanisms indicate which segments of the input sequence the model concentrates on during prediction. We can determine which words or phrases have the greatest influence on the model's output by visualizing attention maps. This is especially helpful when analyzing models for tasks like text summarization or machine translation, when knowing the model's focus aids in explaining the outcomes.

- Saliency Maps: Another essential tool for interpretability are saliency maps. They offer visual signals that demonstrate how particular input components affect the model's output. Saliency maps can be used to show which words or tokens have the greatest influence on a given decision for LLMs when applied to textual inputs. This is particularly helpful in applications like sentiment analysis, where knowing how particular words relate to one another and how that relationship affects sentiment prediction can yield insightful information.

A useful tool for elucidating how each characteristic (or token, in the case of LLMs) contributes to the final prediction is SHAP (Shapley Additive Explanations) values. According to each input's unique contribution, SHAP divides the prediction value among the different inputs. Working with complicated models, where conventional approaches like attention or saliency might not adequately capture the nuanced interactions between the model's inputs and outputs, is where this strategy excels.

Selecting Methods Depending on the Audience and Task

The task at hand and the intended audience will determine the interpretability strategies you use. For instance, attention maps and SHAP values can provide information on the rationale behind each word choice in text generation tasks, where the model generates language that is similar to that of a human. However, saliency maps or LIME (Local

Interpretable Model-Agnostic Explanations) may be more suitable for classification tasks, when the model is making a binary or multi-class choice.

- Task-Oriented Explanation: Select the method that best fulfills the task's objectives. SHAP values, for instance, can explain why specific phrases resulted in the assignment of a given label in document classification, whereas attention maps may offer a more lucid image of how the model extracts important information to produce succinct summaries in text summarization.

- An explanation focused on the audience: Your audience will determine how detailed your explanation should be. You might offer extremely technical insights to developers or data scientists, such as the mathematical underpinnings of SHAP values. Simpler, visual explanations like attention maps or easily comprehensible heatmaps could work better for non-technical stakeholders.

10.2 UI and Dashboards for Explainability

Interactive dashboards and user interfaces (UI) that show model behavior and offer clear insights into its decision-making process are among the most useful techniques to make AI explainability accessible. Dashboards are particularly helpful for stakeholders who need to have faith that the model is making fair, accurate, and explicable judgments but may not have a thorough understanding of machine learning.

Creating Frontends That Stakeholders Can Understand

Presenting intricate models results in an understandable and useful manner is the aim of explainability dashboard design. Among the important factors are:

- Interactive Visualization: Dashboards ought to provide consumers with interactive, real-time visualizations that let them examine how the AI model makes decisions. This can include the option to click on various input components (such words or sentences) to see how they affected the prediction.

- Unambiguous Labels and Explanations: Each visual component on the dashboard should have a clear, succinct explanation. Labels should describe what each area of the attention map represents, for instance, and the accompanying text should explain why some words had a greater influence than others.

- Customizable Views: Various users can require varying degrees of information. The dashboard's usefulness can be improved by offering users customisable views that let them switch between high-level summaries and more in-depth details.

Resources for Explainability Dashboard Construction

Building explainability dashboards for LLMs can be aided by a number of tools:

- Streamlit: Streamlit is a well-known open-source software framework for building machine learning interactive online applications. It is a great option for developing unique dashboards that illustrate the behavior of AI models since it enables quick prototyping and customization.

- Gradio: Gradio provides a user-friendly interface for making interactive machine learning model demonstrations. It is a great tool for developers and end users to interact with model outputs because it can be used to display LLMs and offer real-time interpretability insights.

- Visualization APIs: Dashboards can incorporate APIs like Matplotlib and Plotly to generate unique plots, graphs, and charts that illustrate the inner workings of LLMs. To make these visualizations easier for stakeholders to understand, they can use saliency maps, attention maps, and SHAP plots.

10.3 Including Explainability in the Cycle of Development

Interpretability must be incorporated into the AI development process in order to be genuinely effective. Explainability should be a continuous consideration that is

examined and improved at every level of development, from the first model training to deployment.

From Creation to Implementation: When and What to Test

Models stay transparent and compliant when interpretability is incorporated at every stage of development. Among the crucial phases to think about are:

- Model Training: During training, developers can gain insight into how the model learns to make decisions by using tools such as saliency maps and attention processes. Early behavior analysis of the model allows developers to see any biases or unusual trends in the training set.

- Model Evaluation: Models should be assessed for interpretability using methods such as SHAP or LIME prior to deployment. This guarantees that the model makes decisions in a way that is clear and consistent with expectations.

- Post-Deployment Monitoring: To make sure the model operates as intended, it is essential to continuously monitor its interpretability after it has been deployed. Stakeholders can monitor the model's activity by using dashboards and interactive visualizations to see how it reacts to new inputs.

Using XAI to Interpret Errors and Enhance Prompts

XAI tools can assist in detecting faults in the model's outputs during the development cycle. In cases where the model fails, explainability techniques might help identify the problem. Attention maps and saliency diagrams, for example, can reveal which words or phrases caused a language model to classify a text erroneously. This can direct timely modifications and model optimization, ultimately enhancing performance.

10.4 LLM Interpretability's Future

The demand for more sophisticated interpretability techniques will grow as AI continues to improve. Because of their enormous complexity and scale, LLMs in

particular face specific difficulties. Improving openness, equity, and trust while tackling these issues will be the main goals of LLM interpretability in the future.

Unsolved Issues: Grounding, Summarizing, and Aligning

There are still a number of obstacles to adequately interpreting LLMs:

- Aligning Representations: As LLMs get increasingly complicated, it gets harder to match their internal representations with notions that are understandable to humans. In order to make AI models more interpretable in ways that humans can understand, future research will concentrate on enhancing this alignment.

- Summarizing Model Behavior: It is still difficult to give thorough explanations of model behavior. Although saliency approaches and attention maps offer localized insights, it is still very difficult to generate summaries of complete model actions.

- Grounding Explanations: Another difficulty is placing AI explanations in practical settings. AI models frequently work in abstract spaces, and converting these intricate, high-dimensional areas into language that humans can understand is still a major area of study interest.

The Direction of Research and Your Role in It

The field of LLM interpretability research is still in its infancy, and there are plenty of opportunities to learn more. Innovation is needed in areas like cross-domain explainability, multimodal interpretability, and causal reasoning. By creating novel methods, working with interdisciplinary teams, and expanding the realm of AI transparency, researchers and practitioners can make valuable contributions to the area.

In addition to being a question of ethics and compliance, developing a strong interpretability toolkit is a means of guaranteeing the continued use, dependability, and trustworthiness of AI models especially big language

models. Organizations may make sure that their AI systems are transparent, understandable, and equitable by creating a strong XAI pipeline, incorporating interactive dashboards, and incorporating interpretability throughout the development process. LLM interpretability has a bright future ahead of it, with research spurring innovation and providing fresh approaches to improving the reliability and accessibility of these intricate systems. As researchers and developers, it is our duty to set the standard for making AI accessible to all.

ABOUT THE AUTHOR

 Author and thought leader in the IT field Taylor Royce is well known. He has a two-decade career and is an expert at tech trend analysis and forecasting, which enables a wide audience to understand complicated concepts.

Royce's considerable involvement in the IT industry stemmed from his passion with technology, which he developed during his computer science studies. He has extensive knowledge of the industry because of his experience in both software development and strategic consulting.

Known for his research and lucidity, he has written multiple best-selling books and contributed to esteemed tech periodicals. Translations of Royce's books throughout the world demonstrate his impact.

Royce is a well-known authority on emerging technologies and their effects on society, frequently requested as a

speaker at international conferences and as a guest on tech podcasts. He promotes the development of ethical technology, emphasizing problems like data privacy and the digital divide.

In addition, with a focus on sustainable industry growth, Royce mentors upcoming tech experts and supports IT education projects. Taylor Royce is well known for his ability to combine analytical thinking with technical know-how. He sees a time when technology will ethically benefit humanity.

www.ingramcontent.com/pod-product-compliance
Lightning Source LLC
LaVergne TN
LVHW022350060326
832902LV00022B/4352